Ella Adams

Resolved
A Juxtaposition of Thoughts

Ella Adams

Ella Adams

Dedication

This book is dedicated to Jordan Micah Pinkard;
My Grandson.

"I have no apologies to make to anyone or institution for any of the indictments or hypothesis in this work. For I have carefully examined and thought through each and every one of the poems before they were included in this final work before printing."

-Dr. Yosef A. A. ben-Jochannan: Africa, Mother of Western Civilization

Table of Contents

Ella Adams

The Clay You Are

The Lord sees your life as a ball of clay which is spread out before him on the canvas of life. He sees your life as a process of movements, which He, the Potter, has formed. He stops once in a while to form a juxtaposition of it onto His canvas. With Him at the wheel, the formation becomes a manuscript of love.

As He studies its metamorphosis, He notices the outline of its sinuous curves beginning to form. Their formation and curvatures make Him, the potter, the designer, smiles. He says, "Its hues are what I need." He says, "Its hair texture is perfect."

Suddenly the clay begins to move toward Him as if it were part of a symphony of life that carries sweet lovely melodies of love toward His outstretched arms. But then you notice that His hands never stop moving.

They never stopped forming the work they had begun. The clay He's holding begins to take on character and form. It begins to radiate light and joy. "My," you say, "What a beautiful piece of pottery."

But once you look a little closer you smile
because now you understand that the image
has been you all along.

"My," you say, "He has formed me! I am in
the image of God."

Then you beheld God and you smiled.

Primary

When the doors of life swing open, hurry
through its portal;
When time allows its essence to be captured
by mere mortals.
When the bird of love swoops down on you
when you are reminiscing;
That is when you must relinquish the love
you've held for me.

Him

Cold and moist, cold and dry, his feet always
next to mine throughout the night;
Cold and moist is what my heart felt
whenever our souls would embrace.

Life and death comes and goes is what I have
learned to discern;
Earth and dust was his scent and his strength
was all I needed to incarcerate his essence.
I am he. He's between each breath I speak.

I speak his name as I hold onto my
nakedness. Torn and broken, sink or swim,
mend and fusion;
I will always call out to him.
Pain and sorrow, have called him to his end.

If Only

When there is enough time…
When there is enough time I will fly a kite.
When there is enough time I shall sail the
seven seas in search of you.
When there is enough time I will start looking
after me.
When there is enough time I will save a tree.
When there is enough time I will stop to see
who it was that had been waiting for me.
When there is enough time I will wonder who
it was that really needed me.

And, finally, if there had been enough time, I
would have perceived that it had always been
you who was waiting for me.
And if I had enough time left I would have
spent it letting you love me.

Mirrors

Most of my life I spent looking for you.
Only to have each encounter between us
judged untrue.
I never understood when we touched that our
hearts would deny what we both knew.
So now that I am old, and unable to move, I
realized that the one I had always been
searching for was only you.

Don't Confuse Me with My Ancestor

For the reason that my ancestors were brought here as your uninvited servants and slaves and said nothing about your intrusion into their ways; moreover and because they had to bow to those of lesser age, I won't bow to you nor to you progeny.

Now the fact that they used your discards and never complained I shall not bring any into my domain.
As well as the fact that they allowed themselves to be worked as your ancestor's saw fit into an early grave, I will never walk silently to my annihilation in the span of my days.
Not without first saying and doing all that I can to stop the procession on the way to my end.

On the other hand, I am a descendant of the ancestors I have drawn closer to in my memory.
Ancestors I have come to love, to understand, and to cherish the endowment of pride they left as my heritage.
Hetep – Peace and Happiness.

Obesity

Someone once said to me that I was more
precious than gold.
While others have said that my attributes are
too wonderful to be whole.
Then once I was told that it really did not
matter.
All my life you told me my size was never a
factor.
So why do I feel as though my life has been
shattered whenever you tell me to walk in your
shadow?

Derailment of Our Youth

Something is wrong and I want to cry.
My heart is sad. They are going to die.
Why should I feel remorse at their plight when
they can easily take my life?
Is it their youth, or is it the prospect of a better
tomorrow that keeps me fighting for their
lives?

Ella Adams

His Execution

Bring him here to me, in the darkness of his
dreams;
Allow me the privilege of protecting his
essence as he sleeps.
In hope that the root of his feelings drifts back
to me;
Let me be the one who keeps his spirit safe and
free.

Save him and keep him safe I implore you my
dreams;
Acknowledge his suffering as a breeze,
brushed by the steel wrapped around his heels.
He waits for the decree from his guards;
The he looks at the light shining on his soul
from his suckling to his sleep.

Stolen Thoughts

All that you have taken from me you who call
yourself Europe's seed;
From the tops of the pyramids to the bottom of
the seas, you found my ancestors sleeping in
peace.

From the rolling hills of countries now
deceased.
To the depths of Death Valleys you came
creeping to me.

So that I might bow down to thee
You stole the life that was given me and feed it
to your offspring
Now they are here standing before me;
healthy, strong, and free, desiring to be the
masters of my seed.

Morning

Spring comes; dawn breaks upon the face of
the saints as they awake.
Warmth shines, tides breakthrough onto my
lover's slumbering face
For you are always awakened by each breath
the day makes.
Nature glows as hearts explored upon the
earth's landscape.
My longing for your embrace is more than my
heart can take.

Illumination

They can say to me until the moon descends
that you had never been.
When they said my heart must make amends
before my time here ends.
Even though I know, I watched as your
footprints disappeared beneath the desert sand.

So, while the night is a glow by your wisdom
you had left behind, I continue to watch as
your essence illuminate the path as it leads me
closer to mines.

The sand castle on our mound in the sky where
you are reflecting in the wind of my mind will
slip away after time.
I can still hear them saying that I had imagined
the love I felt deep inside my soul.
Nevertheless, my darling, I will love you until
there's no sand between my toes.

Lost Youth

I see them moving through this maze.
I see them changing day by day.
Into what I dare not say as I brush my fears
away.
I see them standing too close, too near, to
wants, to thrills.
Then I release my tears.

My Identify Knowing

I know you are wondering is there more.
I know you are wondering what all this is for.
I hear you saying help me please.
I know there is something more for me.
Something I won't have to fear.
Something I could always declare.
Now I know you are wondering if I am still
listening.

His Breath

Day after day I think of you and though we
have never met;
Day after day I cry for you and even though
your heart escaped its final fate.
Your breath was released upon the reservoir of
my soul;
It was left to wither and to die within the
darkness of the night.
Your breath was vaporized within the mist of
the early morning light.
Today, I wondered what was in your eyes.

Exit

The weight that weighs upon me is very old.
And the grief of lost days has torn a hole deep
within my soul.
The gifts given to me to mend the rifts have
themselves left a deep penetrating wound in
the middle of my essence.
But when the sun comes up in the morning my
heart reaches for its tenderness and drinks
again of its nectar of reunion and regeneration.
Then the rips and the tears no longer are of
importance.

Transformed

Darkness has swept down upon my people as
the history of our mother has now been
replaced by that of our stepfathers'.
First he taught us how to hate the eyes of our
mother.
Then he destroyed the love we kept buried
deep within borders of each other.
Her words are now lost within the texts on his
press.
Her colors which once covered our nakedness,
has now been bleached by the propaganda of
his contempt.
Her essence and love that was once reached for
by all, receives a mere gesture from those she
calls in the night.
Today her children show much admiration for
their stepfather's message as their character is
being castrated.
Still she calls out to them to turn towards her
once again.
But while she waits, she weeps as her memory
is being swept from the repositories of their
judgment as their stepfather continues to feed
them lies from his provision.

What about My Brother

What about my brother?
Why does he lie and cheat his brother?
Could it be for the mother's daughter of his
master's seed?
And can it be said that he has shown his true
colors in the mist of my adversity?
And will his women folk, speak kindly of his
deeds?
As he searches for a new identity, please tell
me what has happened to my brother's love for
his sister; me?
Was it the gold or the color of her mother that
stole the soul of my brother from me?
And will my brother ever fulfill the promises
he once made to his father's seed?

His House

I remember when we were in our infancy the
day your father stole my virginity.
It was also the moment I began my quest to
gain enough strength to denounce the love
which your father requested
I knew that my need and plea to be free from
the start, was enough to release the beast that
dwelled deep within his bravery.
It was only when I began to pray for my
mother's seed that I was able to be set free
from the hold that your father had on me.

And today you see it is no longer a mystery
why your mother was able to reject your
father's seed.
And although the years have set me free, I
have often remembered what your father did to
me in his beginning.
At which point my heart immediately cries out
for his humanity.

The Dew

All that you have belongs to me, you who call
yourself Europe's seed.
All that I own you took from me, you who had
no identity.
Many of my vessels which had my seed, you
shattered upon the open sea;
Along with their substance which held our
destiny.
The others you took across the sea wrapped in
your Holy Men's garments of deceit. Where
they are now unable to sprout and harvest for
me because of lies they continue to masticate.

Release

My words are in jail, can't you tell?
They have been captured and tossed into a cell
by the very men and women who taught me to
spell;
And by those who taught me the difference
between heaven and hell.
But my words are not alone there in their cells;
You see, my books of poetry beat them there.
So, while visiting my friends locked in their
cells, they told of the oath they made to free
them from their hell.
Now by reading this poem you have promised
to help set my enlightenment free.

Troubled

How can I maintain an upright position as I
attempt to find a calm place to glide across this
sea of capitalism?
And how can I build a structure that will float
that will not sink as others have when they had
fallen beneath the quagmire of this system of
loathing lies?
What skills should I search for and capture as
mines as I am attempting to construct a vessel
that will keep my soul from drifting too far on
either side.
I need a vessel that will keep me afloat in the
mist of the wreckage which pushes against my
hopes.
I watched the waves of life rise around me as I
am tossed from side to side on this sea
annihilation.
So will you tell me how one is to survive in
this sea of disinterest which tossed me from
side to side?

Indictments

Bellows of indictments screamed out at him as
he climbed those rickety stairs which pointed
the way to his end.
He never mastered any task given to him
screamed his brother.
As his feet flopped onward towards his shelter;
He never did anything right like a man shouted
another.
Then he sought the hand of his brother, hoping
to get strength enough to keep on fighting.
He never realized he was getting close to the
edge cried out another as his pace increased as
he was hoping for something better.
I knew he would not become anything cried
out his father. Just then he turned in time to see
the hate in the eyes of his co-worker.
It would have been better if his mother had
decided on another, said the man with his
collar opposite the others.
Then when he turned the corner on the last
strides before his end, he looked once more to
see where it had all began.
With his hand on the door which held in
reserve his hopes, freedom and love he never
un-earth a familiar voice said come in. I
forgive you my son.
The table is prepared for you.

It was at that moment the switch was pulled which released him from his life of disappointment into the lovely arms of his savior.

Mother's Hope

Skin grown rough from the year of deep
sorrow as one watched and hoped for a better
tomorrow.
Weak and ejected of hope and joy she sat and
watched their dreams being destroyed.
For years she carried her pain in silence which
had only left behind silence and shame.
She sat and wondered what would have been if
their yesterdays could have been their
tomorrows.

First Impression

What must I do to win your trust?
Does it matter to you that I am hurt?
How may I answer each time you call?
For today is the day you cut me out of your
heart.
Who said I said I wished to be you?
Who have helped to protect my identity?
And where must I tread for you to see that I
have always been free?

Once Again

Toxins and poisons were gifts we each
collected.
While the thought of a life devoid of our hearts
shouted, I love you, from inside their love
quarters.
Rot and fragments of hurts not mended had
commenced to go bad and begun to seep
through their defenses.
Visions of dreams had started and stopped-
they were quickly blown away by the
continued damage caused by the poison
dripping into their hearts.

My Love's Heart

Who's going to take care of my heart when I
am gone?
Will it be a loved one or someone from afar?
Who will take over what I have left undone, on
the day of my moving on?
I ask you, will you be in charge of my lover's
needs, and on the day my name is resounding
throughout the seas?
Or, will you stand by and just watch me leave?

Grandfather

I wish I knew you when I was young.
I wish you were there for me to swing from
your arms.
I wish my feet had walked throughout your
home.
I wish that I could have smelled your cologne
to keep it sealed deep in my heart because I
know his scent would still be lingering on.
I wish I could have watched as you played
your horn on those long, hot summer days to
keep your voice forever being heard.
Oh, how I wished dear Grandfather, that I had
been there the day you were called home to be
with the Lord.

My Pet

Since you came into my life I no longer
wonder aimlessly through the park.
Knowing you will always be there waiting
anxiously for me to return.
You allowed me to taste unconditional love for
the first time in my life.
Knowing that you are my best friend for life,
one who will always be here by my side; let's
me release my loneliness gently into the sky.

I Miss You

Feelings are what branches us from our
yesterdays, whenever our tomorrows try to
force themselves into our today.
Just like the times between our winters and our
springs remind us that our fall is only moments
away.
Maybe just maybe that is all of the time we
should have together before our reality
awakens us to our own restricted captured
minds.

Who Am I

I am who I am I am not it.
I am who I am I am not them.
I am who I am I am not the other.
I am who I am I am not those…
I am who I am I am not last.
I am who I am I am not sorry.
I am who I am I am not lazy.
I am who I am I am not sin.
I am who I am I am not unteachable.
Who I am is a reflection of who I should be
and will become.
What I am doing is what I must.
Because who and what I am, I am.

The Ring

A warm breeze from an evening wind swept
by my tear stained cheeks the day I gave you
back your rings.
As my heart released its pain of our lost love
on my face;
I tasted the guilt I hoped it would cause drip
down my face.
Today I stopped time and again began to
wonder how it all had ended.
Never could I have dreamed that you my love
would do this to me.
And to think your inappropriateness came to
me in a dream.
My tears which were torn from my heart are
now in capsulate in this tragic love story of
loss.

Ella Adams

Born and raised in California, Author Ella Adams now makes her home in Texas. She currently holds a Master's Degree in Psychology and a Counseling Degree from Texas A&M University.
Adams is a novelist, journalist, and also the creator of board and card games.

Ella Adams

Acknowledgements

To my God and Savior Jesus Christ who gave me the ability to see beyond my own limited intellect to be able to grasp His heart.
To My Children Horace and Gail, my two best friends who encouraged me to follow my destiny. To all of those whom shoulders I now stand because without their fearlessness I would not have met my Savior.
A special thanks to my editor and publisher TiTi Ladette whose own journey of discovery led our paths to cross.

Ella Adams